GIRLZ-R-STOO-PID

and

BOYZ-R-DUH-M

OBSERVATIONS OF AN UNBIASED TRAVELER

BY **RAY "LEFTY" RHODES**

DEDICATION

This book is dedicated to my mother because she not only introduced me to but insisted on me having a relationship "at all times" with the truth. She always told me, "Everything in life has consequences good or bad, but if you lie to me, I'm going to whoop yo ass!" She also said, that she'd "rather be respected than loved" because she didn't believe it was possible to be cheated on if you were truly respected.

SPECIAL THANKS

RIP Stanford Walton who taught me how to be a man by leading by example. Cooking, cleaning, working, hustling, grinding and taking full care of my mom and "someone else's kid" as they say today. She kept her check while he paid bills, and he also helped me with homework, taught me to cook, clean and be a man all before she even got home from work.

Also RIP to my Papa Charlie as well. He was THE true definition of a MAN. Married to my grandmother until his death, served his family, his city, his country, and the church! He owned property real estate and the only single family home on the block. We (the family) love and miss you both!

RIP to "Micheal J. Penn" he taught me about how important having a wife was. Men must be a man of GOD to be blessed with a wife and females must be a wife and be accessible to a man of GOD to find a righteous husband.

ACKNOWLEDGEMENTS

First and foremost, I have to acknowledge and pay homage to the man who is responsible for this book; my friend, my cousin, and my mentor as an author and publisher; the ever so patient Samuel Holloway III, or as I will ALWAYS call him... my cousin Robert!

I also HAVE TO acknowledge my female best friends I've had in my life that have been brutally honest about life and relationships.

My sister from another mister when I first got to Minnesota, Nina. We went through the most relationship drama as teens and grew a lot as family. I'm so proud of the woman you've become!

My running partner and soul survivor sister, Blu, we learned so much together in the streets, we STILL here!

RIP to my little sister 6 who woke me up to my thoughtlessness in relationships. I'll NEVER forget you or what you taught me!

My "Ex baby Mama", Ashley, who showed me who I was and how much better I could be. I will ALWAYS remember and appreciate our life together.

My co-founder and 1st ever General manager of DHE, Miss Lena, who showed and proved to me what REAL friends do and what Real love was... you da you da BEST!

Of course in a league of her own I have to acknowledge my 1 and ONLY biological sister Key Killa, my rock my reminder ... My TWIN, thank you SO much for ALWAYS having my back!

Last, but DEFINITELY never least, my Hunny Bunny, the most honest, loyal, and outgoing friend I've EVER had PERIOD!

PROLOGUE

Picture it, a very happy business man is celebrating the opening of his 10th business. With glasses in the air he says, "I stayed single, I stayed hungry, I stayed self-motivated and I stayed focused."

The CEO of multiple companies stares off in a daze, while reminiscing after being asked why he said single first.

He thinks back to how other people he'd known had invested in each other and families and other people kids and friends, but he just stayed focused on him and his goals. As he adds up his sacrifices as compared to the ones asking, he says, as if right then sharing his instant epiphany and realization.

He mentally rejoins the room and they ask him again "how did you do it".

He says I stayed single and self-motivated, therefore I stayed focused!

When they ask why he said "Single first," he stares off into space, remembering his first understanding of what being single meant. His grandmother was at the table doing taxes, and both his grandfather and his mother were at work. He was about 5 or 6 years old at the time and asked if they would file for his mom or would his mom have to file separately. His grandmother said that she and his grandfather filed as married and that his mom filed as single. She also told him that he would be considered single until he got married. She went onto say that everything married people have, they share but when you're single you're only responsible for you and your kids if you have them. The boy thought to himself, *I'll be single with no kids until I have everything I want!*

He was already raised as an only child so he kept that mindset and never fully invested in a relationship. He grew up seeing people unhappy with their job and their mates so he stayed single,

self-motivated and stayed focused because he saw
that:

"GIRLZ ARE S-TOO-PID
AND BOYZ ARE DUH-M.

INTRODUCTION

Being the son of a psych nurse has made me a very observant person. One of my favorite pastimes is people watching. Being a paid traveling performer for 10 years, owning my own company and going to college, I've paid attention to how people interact with each other in countless environments when it comes to relationships. I've concluded that GIRLZ are S-TOO-PID and BOYZ are DUH-M.

Life experiences through my eyes are that GIRLZ are S-TOO-PID and BOYZ are DUH-M. It's a story about the unrealistic expectations that people have and put onto others when entering "situationships." BOYZ are looking for shells and GIRLZ are looking for actors.

My papa Charlie retired Lead Detective of Robbery and Homicide in Chicago. He and my grandmother owned property and buildings including the one I grew up in. I was the first-born grandchild. We'd sit on the Westside of Chicago and he'd explain gentrification and their plans and concepts that would shape our future as Americans.

My mom was his first born and favorite child which is what would always bond us. Given that quick fact and being the 1st born to a mother who happened to be a Psych Nurse for 30 years, I tend to be a little more observant in my day to day activities.

Being a traveling paid performer, I see a lot of different people and places. Remaining single and staying focused has gotten me all I have and to where I am today! Now, being that I've been a TV/Music Producer, a writer, a cameraman, a recording artist, a manager, and a performer, something I've noticed over the last decade of my moving around playing fly on the wall is that GIRLZ R S-TOO-PID and BOYZ R DUH-M! I pray this book will help generations mature, Americans grow, and the world an overall better place for everyone.

TABLE OF CONTENTS

CHAPTER 1

LIL GIRLZ

If you wonder why I said GIRLZ are S-TOO-PID first, it's because I'm a gentleman and I always believe ladies are first. Little girls are taught in America that they are princesses and they should be treated like princesses and they're taught that there is a prince charming out there just perfect for them that'll cater to all their emotions, needs, he's a perfect gentleman, he doesn't cheat, doesn't look at other girls, along with a number of other perfect bullshit.

First, that's what little girls grow up believing that they are still a princess. Rather it be a single parent or a two-parent household, they (American Parents) raise their son to be a king and their daughter to be a princess. In America (being a predominately white place of power, of influence, and all of that) there is no woman of power who has superseded her counterpart in history as far a white woman, since the time of Amelia Earhart, and not even HER but you get the picture!

No disrespect intended, just proving points. Elanor Roosevelt was married to a president, Jackie Onassis was married to a president and Marilyn Monroe was fucking some of everybody and married to some of everybody. Hillary Clinton had Bill Clinton, he was a president. No white wife ever superseded her counterpart and been celebrated by history. I guess that IS the 1st of 48 laws!

★ ★ ★ ★ ★ ★

Growing up in an age and era where divorce was/is publicly announced and socially accepted, I never saw a truly happy married couple. The Cosby's didn't make sense to me because what does a Doctor and a Lawyer have in common besides massive student loans, plus with school and work when would they have time for each other or the kids. It just wasn't realistic to me and all married people that I saw actually "settled" for marriage and it was okay to give up on your dreams for a family. Lol... you only settle when you can't win.

I believe both spouse can only be truly happy together after reaching personal goals. Nobody wants to be a part of your half ass life. Misery loves company so nowadays, people are too lazy to educate and elevate therefore they choose to congregate and subsequently how we as Americans tend to populate.

Even in High School, I saw boys investing more in girls than in themselves, more than their education, their family, and their money. Girls make their lives about the boys and the boys make their lives about boys. (Friends, family, gang members, teammates, video game partners, celebrities, or their coworkers and or boss are all other boys they give their time to instead of the girl.)

AmeriKKKA brainwashes us to think of white history or the whites POV as American history which would make the white man ruler and the white woman his queen. But there is only one queen and she's in England. Therefore, since they "trump" (no pun intended) other "races" (only 1 race, HUMAN) then white women here are only known as, and can only be, princesses! Even the president's wife is known as 1st lady, how about Woman in Chief, ijs.

Elanor Roosevelt, Hilary Clinton, Anna Nicole Smith, Cher, OJS Nicole, Marilyn Monroe, Ozzy Wife, LOL, white girls play the background good because white men are the ULTIMATE Amerikk-kan oppressors.

Obama (real) African-American (White). In most other countries the women are submissive (that's what they teach us here) and here, American is known as white (the image they project). Never outshine the "Master!"

★ ★ ★ ★ ★ ★

Little girls are growing up never to grow up. They are always stuck in a little girl mind. That's why the first chapter is about little girls. That's what people need to realize; it's why you're little girls in my mind...because you are little girls in your own minds and Amerikkka's eyes. This is chapter one and everything that falls into this chapter are examples I give of why. If you want someone to treat you like a little girl, that means that there are daddy issues there starting off like everybody in America.

You must get out of the little girl mentality if you want a relationship. The first thing is realizing you're not a little girl. Grow the fuck up and be a grown ass woman. There is no prince charming out there!

CHAPTER 2

LIL BOYZ

Adult males are little BOYZ in their heads. (reference Dr. Frances Cress Wesling's quotes and theory most notably mentioned in the beginning of the movie "Baby Boy") Most adult males that are trying to be in relationships or end up in relationships, have a situation going on and just need help, they're not looking for a partner. They are ONLY looking for HELP! They are not bringing anything to the table emotionally, they're just looking at who has the best table to sit at, that's what little boys do.

A man builds a foundation, builds a house, protects, and provides security, that's what a man does. Little boys go around trying to find tables to sit at, get them a quick meal, don't even clean up behind themselves, and takes off running outside wanting to PLAY.

As far as commitment; a grown man knows how to commit, little boys just don't know how to. Little boys don't have any bills in their names, no permanent address, no cars or insurance in their name, no jobs, no careers, no contracts, no post education. That's little boy shit and that's why little boys are DUH-M.

I spell out duh-m because little Boyz don't think. They don't take time to learn and don't take care of themselves, like DUH. Just DUH-M. Boys are DUH-M because they're boys in their minds. They think with their dicks. Boys want to hang with their boys, boys want girls to act like boys, boys want a girl that do what they like to do, and that's selfish shit. That's why little boys are dumb, because they don't know what they want and girls are stupid because they are trained to think that they are still little girls, so they stupid and fuck their whole shit up.

Little boys are DUH-M because they want what they're not willing to give. All they want is want, want, want, like little boys. That's all little boys do is want, and want someone else to clean up their shit.

CHAPTER 3

S-TOO-PID

This is why I say girls are S-TOO-PID, this is why I hyphened out S-TOO-PID. I didn't spell it literally correct because I'm NOT calling girls stupid. What I'm stating is that you're S-TOO-PID, like you TOO-PID! Let me break it down, girls are complex, more complex than boys so that's what actually meant by S-TOO-PID. Girls lie to themselves when it comes to their emotions. Your emotions can make you say, "I feel like" this. However, that's not truth.

Whenever you're dealing with emotions, that's not the facts. You can state that even though it's 98 degrees, it feels like it's 68 degrees. Fuck your feelings, deal with facts. You must accept the facts before you start talking about your emotions and feelings. You must admit the facts to yourself. It doesn't feel like he's cheating, he's fucking cheating! Point being: stop going through complicated emotions to go around or not deal with the facts and truth.

My grandfather retired lead Detective of robbery and homicide in Chicago and started off as a patrolman walking the beat so i know for a fact that being a detective is a full time and very professional job. Girls try to put together patterns that don't exist. They try to say, "He does this all the time so, this means that he likes me, this means He s cheating, this means that he ready for marriage, this means that he wants to have a child with me, this means He's lying, this means that he wants a family, he said that he wanted a family so obviously he's ready to have sex and start having babies."

NO!

"Oh, he said he wanted to have a family someday soon so obviously he's going to pop the question!"

NO!

The most important thing between any two people is a clear verbal communication. CLEAR VERBAL COMMUNICATION! This is why I say girls are S-TOO-PID because they go through complicated lengths to have misunderstandings and miscommunications instead of just asking.

When a girl asks a boy a question, she says, "Oh so this?"

And he says, "NO!"

And she says, "Oh, so what you're saying is, that?"

And he says, "NO!"

NO! Nobody ain't saying shit! Ask him a simple question and let him answer!

★ Clear Verbal Understanding ★

That's what S-TOO-PID is about. It's a complex way of causing, creating and adding to a problem. Therefore, I say girls are S-TOO-PID because they create their own problems. They create them with their unnecessary complex thinking, emotions and feelings. And with them already thinking that they're little girls, so they expect him to protect them, to take care of them, they expect him to do all of these things when it's very unreasonable to expect that from a man who is not your husband, he is not your father, he's not your king, you're not a princess, and you're not even royalty baby, ok, you're being S-TOO-PID!

CHAPTER 4

DUH-M

Boys are DUH-M, I say DUH-M and I spelled it like that because they're dumb. Most boys don't have a reason to cheat, they don't have a reason to do a lot of the things they do. Boys lie for no reason, they lie when there aren't even consequences and nobody asked them. Boys are DUH-M because they do shit like leave the toilet seat up, piss all over the floor, that's DUH-M shit.

It's the same thing as training an animal, and you see that an animal is acting like that and you know that an animal does S-TOO-PID shit like mess up your house. Boys think that it's okay to go to a strip club when you're in a relationship without your girl. If you're girl cool going to a strip club and ya'll are together, then ya'll go together. Girls tell you that, "Oh yea it's okay baby if you want to go to the strip club" and yo DUH-M ass go to the strip club.

Boys are also DUH-M because they want to hang out with their boys, they want to do boy shit. That's just DUH-M, when you're ready to be a man and you want to have a woman, then the bible even tells you, "You put away your childish things", when the man wants to join and have a family with his woman then that man is supposed to separate from his family to begin and start his own branch of family and his wife takes the place of his mother. That's who you should be taking care of and be ready to do. And if you're not ready to do that, then you're just DUH-M for wasting your own time. You could be working on being a man but instead you're trying to shack up because that's what little boys do (that comes from Steve Harvey's book, I got it from the movie)

DUH-M because you're supposed to be a leader, you're supposed to be the head of your household. When you're a man you're supposed to be a protector, you're supposed to be all of this, you're supposed to be the head of your family.

If not, then you're just too DUM-H to lead and you're just a little boy. If you need help to lead and you need someone else to tell you to that you have to lead your family, then here you go... you have to be a fucking man. If you want your family to go to church, you take your family to church, you want your family in mosque, you take your family to mosque, you want your family to go camping, you take your family fucking camping. When you provide for and you protect your family as a fucking man, then you're a man but if not then you're just a little boy and a DUM-H one at that!

CHAPTER 5

UNREALISTIC

This goes for boys and girls, they're both unrealistic which is why they're not growing! You are a man and you are a woman but you're still being a boy and you're still being a girl. Until you HAVE to FIX those things about yourself as little girls and little boys and come to a real reality of the world, accept your reality and then work TOGETHER as GROWN UP ADULTS in the REAL world to be a better you and fix yourself. There is no half and half. You BOTH have to be 100%.

It's unrealistic to think I got half and you have half so we can be whole together. NO! That's not how it works. You need to be a whole person and the other person does too, then you all can be better together. You end up being a new person when you are in a relationship. You're not you anymore, you put the "U" in "US" and now it's "WE"!

We are new people! We eat sushi, when I didn't eat sushi. I know that because now I tried it because I was with you and we tried something together. We go to new places together; when we get a place, we get all new furniture for our place. We have better credit together than what we have separate. We know how much debt we have and what we accumulated together.

That's what's unrealistic about people, they don't want to accept their own shit, fix their own shit, and then be able to say, "This is who I am, this is what I like!" That's what's unrealistic. You don't even know yourself, so how in the fuck can you introduce yourself to ANYBODY else? How can I love you for you when you don't even know who you are? You haven't introduced you to me and you haven't been real with who you are. So, it's very unrealistic to think that anybody could ever fucking love you.

★ ★ ★ ★ ★ ★

I knew this lady who was an unemployed, abusive, loud, ignorant, drunk crackhead but was super fun and let her kids have most of what they wanted like pets, but didn't provide them with all of what they needed like a real mother should. All I ever saw the father do was go to work and drink. When the father moved out, then the mother got with another man and the same thing happened.

I remember Tina and Ken were crack smokers I knew and for years Tina smoked crack and Ken smocked weed but eventually both were smoking crack and then there was Jojo and Kenny. Same situation and Jojo and Kyle. Now JoJo is Married to Kenny and they're BOTH sober and I'm proud of them. Pops (RIP CED) and Mama Wanda were on drugs, on hustles, and eventually worked to be sober together and be better grandparents than parents. I love and am proud of BOTH of y'all and the example you set that it's never too late to change your life and be a positive influence on your family and community!

I caught a DUI went to classes and they told me that 90 something percent of people on drugs were lead to or introduced by the opposite sex. I'd conclude that relationships lead you to drinking, drugs, jail and death. Not even celebs can become power couples for life and to me all that equals is there is no success in relationships. All we have is Will and Jada, God bless they souls.

Until you have what you want, then you have no real time, money or emotion for anybody else. You must get to know someone in order to know what they like. So, what happens when you spend time and money just to find out someone doesn't like you enough or maybe just not as much as you like them? What about common goals and family? Think about health problems and personal beliefs and of course religion!

IF you invest in yourself as much/every time you invest in others, THEN how much more would you have?! That's how much you're taking away from yourself. You have a deadline and an expiration date on this earth. Therefore, people say they wasted their lives on other people or ungrateful friends and good for nothing kids who put them in homes because they can't or refuse to take care of them!

People don't get you places, you get where you got to go, and people stay around. What are you bringing when expecting your level of standards? Don't be an unrealistic boy or girl, grow up!

Quit being DUH-M & S-TOO-PID!

CHAPTER 6

EXPECTATIONS

Boys and girls both have expectations that they're not willing to meet themselves. Boys want girls that have a flat stomach and have this and have that when they don't go to the gym themselves. They don't work out AT ALL. These are the boys that want girls like that. Boys that don't have a job, want girls that have a job. Boys that don't have a car, want girls with a car. Boys that don't won't this want girls to have that.

Now girls on the other hand, will have 3 fucking kids by 4 different dudes, "Yea I said that" but they want a dude with no kids. Girls that don't sell drugs want a dude that sells drugs. Girls that don't gang bang, want a nucca that gang bang. Girls problems as far as their expectations are they expect a prince charming, they expect a guy to be someone who that they don't know how to be. Furthermore, they expect him to know how to be perfect to them when they haven't shared or taught him what it takes because most likely she don't even know herself (how to be happy and what makes her happy)!

★ ★ ★ ★ ★ ★

I noticed my grandpa was working but grandma was shopping. I had boys pay me to do girls homework but not theirs. I lost my virginity at the age of seven years old to a 10 year old, I caught my first pistol case at 12, I had my first car at 13, I was a popular cool kid in high school so I've always been and had so many "coochie magnets," that I've probably peeped more game than any one human has ever ran themselves.

I first moved to Minneapolis I was 17, foot working (a freestyle street style of dancing originated in Chicago) never danced or rapped in Chicago. I got to Minneapolis with no supervision but plenty of understanding of how the hood, drug empires, pimping, the game, and the streets worked. However, in Minneapolis, the people in the streets didn't know the rules to the game as I was taught, so I became a consultant to many hustlers in the streets. Worked for a division of Microsoft at 18 and was at AT&T global before 21. From the streets to corporate America and from jail cells to college campuses rather crackhead or CEOs I've seen first hand that your status, ethnicity, or pay grade/job title doesn't change the fact that you GIRLZ R S-TOO-PID AND BOYZ R DUH-M for having such unrealistic expectations! Boyz will do anything or nothing to get a female and GIRLZ will do anything to keep what they have!

Relations I've had started at seven years old with a ten year old by the name of Danielle. She was calling her mom boyfriend name because that's what she saw or heard her mom doing. I'll never forget it, we lived at 1170 West Erie, Chicago, IL and it all started because she had something I wanted, a Nintendo! We made a trade and I expected to be compensated from that day forward after losing my virginity!

At eight years old my mom, the nurse, showed me a video and diseases in books and I will never forget syphilis pictures of the back. I think she expected me to stop after knowing the severity of the situation and consequences to having sex. I started trying to have sex at 10 years old, but always safely, as much as I could. By 12/13, I was driving and smashing on a regular. I expected to be good at sex from the experience and expected to get it on a regular and from whoever because of what I understood my "status" to be.

My uncles took me to the strip clubs when I graduated high school. I was crazy and popular. I modeled for "Pro Scout" right around the time when Sean William Scott aka "Stiffler" (from American Pie) rose to stardom from the same agency, then my mom got me paid to go on proms and homecomings from older ladies who wanted their daughters to be escorted and not sexed on. I was known as a gentleman, smashed like crazy on their loose friends and family members. I ended up being a hoe magnet and hustled with hoes but never really pimped as a profession.

My mom taught me "if you know how to tell the truth, you never have to lie." It had just so happened that "squares" couldn't handle the rudeness of my truth but hoes loved it and were attracted to the raw delivery in which I exercised.

After meeting my first white girlfriend in college I felt victimized and here was a female that shared the homie view and I started to look at my daughter's mother differently when the blood test proved that the child wasn't mine. After the friendship dissolved, the relationship was over, and I said fuck it, it's over. Never realizing that when you break up with a girl you live with then you're planning on moving out or choosing to be homeless. So, there I was as a full-time employee and college student and part time hustler and homeless.

Simultaneously, my soon to be ex had her ex fucking up her parent's property which was where she was living so she moved in with one of her pregnant friends who wasn't due for six months which gave her long enough to stack for her place let her get out of her situation ASAP and also helped her friend on money while having an extra room. Long story short, she was sucking and fucking on me with another mans seed growing inside of her just like the shit that she said was so trifling and disrespectful about now my ex baby mother. So after giving up my home, my family and most importantly, my friend for this trifling bitch left and kept me with a vendetta that grew into a long-time grudge and unknowing hatred.

However, she was one of the freakiest, most down, loyal, passionate and intense lovers I'd ever seen, heard about and ever had still to this day. She could never understand why I not only hated her but most importantly, why I wouldn't let her love me! After her, I had three blood tests come back negative from females that were just plain lying on who they baby daddy was. One time, I was locked up and got in fights because two girls said I got them pregnant, but they had boyfriends at the time. **SMFH, LITTLE GIRLZ**

My college girlfriend FELT she was better and different than my ex because she had an abortion and never planned on having the baby, as opposed to my ex who knew and lied the entire time. She expected me to love her because she was showing and proving her love for me.

All my friends were dead or locked up and I was constantly going back and forth to jail. Michael J Penn told me how important a wife was, but Papa Charlie said don't let nobody know how much money you have but no other advice. The only way to a successful relationship is in GOD's path that HE sets for you.

I expected things to be easier because of my advantages of soaking up game from so many others. I soon learned that life is YOURS to live and everybody is an individual! Stanford Walton (RIP) taught me how to really treat a woman. He chopped up fresh veggies and even sandwiches had fresh pickles and lettuce! My armed police officer grandfather and thuggish enforcer known convict of a cousin named Buck put my dad Stan out even though he wasn't selling anything out of mom's crib, he cooked, cleaned, worked, hustled and grinded. He helped me with my homework, had her bath water ready and all by the time she was off work. They just heard that he was a dealer so he had to go. They expected better from my mom and never took the time to ask or care about her situation. You're family has expectations when it comes to your relationships as well.

Moms knew what to expect from Sco but the situation still didn't go as planned due to some drastic life-altering unforeseen circumstances, so nothing is guaranteed. He was arrested and sentenced to over 20 years on his first offense while my mom was 8 months pregnant and moving to MN. #1 always has to be #1 because who is going to look out for #1?!

Uncle Daniel was with Christina when she got pregnant with Danisha, went to school at Trane, Certified getting paid and Danisha got half the check. Uncle D used to do karate, graffiti, and ride dirt bikes and now one kid takes half and the other kids before marriage got the other half and now he has kids from marriage, too.

So, I saw that kids will suck all your money out or at least that's what I expected them to do. Later I learned that it didn't/doesn't matter if they're smart, athletic, and active like I was, and your parents have to pay for the equipment transportation and programs or if the child is special needs and it takes more because there's another option of bad ass kids that you'll have to pay for restitution and rehab so understand that I EXPECT children to cost A LOT of MONEY!

Uncle Kip has had legitimate money from the jump and still no kids! Started off as camera man for OPRAH in the '80s then became one of the originators of intranet! He flew me down to Atlanta and put me on to investments and bona fide business company protocol and tax IDs EINs and the fact that I needed school and that's what made me go back for music business and audio production.

He bought me my first suit, shoes, belt and all. He taught me the right way to go about it. My younger cousin Juju went to Robert Morris and he had him riding new Benz and taught him golfing giving him stock tips and putting him on to foreign currency.

I was always rewarded for good behavior and been able to profit from positivity so that always guided my focus when observing options. I knew I didn't have to break the law to get money but any-way if you can't reward your kid for good then they won't be as motivated to do right in the face of wrong like easy money and some crimes even the ones that seem victimless because they are going be prewired to want to work. I work a lot and expect to get paid a lot! Don't let schools out reward you as a parent and don't let the world out teach you when it comes to YOUR child, "free" TV is COST-ING morals! Expect and WORK to be the major influence in your child's life but NEVER the only one.

Females control the situation! You don't make the baby by yourself but you'll have the baby by yourself, so these are your steps of opportune responsivity; if you don't know, condoms (on both sides) swallow, spit, birth control, morning after pill, abortion, and/or adoption, now you know!

You don't have life insurance on him, what if he dies, now your kid has no dad and doesn't know his dad side of the family because you don't even know them! Expect to get to know a person you want to be with BEFORE deciding to bring another mouth to feed into this world expecting help from the government and sympathy from others!

★ ★ ★ ★ ★ ★

The numbers don't look good in that market (happy marriages) so why would I invest?! People want a holy matrimony without a relationship with GOD. People are impressed by looks and resumes but a relationship is a job you don't get paid for and is supposed to be fully invested in for life.

"Girls are like monkeys they never let one branch go until they have a firm grip on another."

—*All About the Benjamins*

Girls meet a new guy and kiss him while actively sucking another guys dick then when the new guy finds out he doesn't want her, but the other guy don't trust her anymore now she's not special to either one. Expect the respect that you show yourself!

Girls say they do things to guard their feelings and protect their heart. But your feelings are always involved so now you're living a lie. You should be happy SOLO then adding another person you'll be even happier! Basically, right now, you're just lying to yourself!

Now he's not an addition to your happiness but you are dependent on him for happiness. Now you want to know where he at, what he is doing, who he fucking and is he thinking about you as much as anything else and or as much as you try.

★ ★ ★ ★ ★ ★

Boys and girls expect everything to change once they get into a relationship. Girls expects guys to become more respectful. They think guys aren't going to look at other girls, they think that guys are not going to go to strip clubs, they think they're not going to do these other things before they weren't in a relationship but there were no boundary lines laid down.

This is the thing about expectations, you must have boundaries. There must be some type of lines, a clear line that both of you know not to cross. This is why it's so important to know yourself. You can't have these expectations like I don't expect this person to drink and drive, but you know this person is a bartender and they drink at work and after work. Plus, you know that they drive themselves to and from work! You just sound S-TOO-PID, quit acting DUH-M!

You can't have expectations of people, like "my girl is a stripper and she does private shows and sucks a little dick in the back room sometimes". "But now that we are together, I expected her to quit the club." Guys expect girls to stop going out and stop having fun and stop having other friends most of the time, that's what boys expect.

Boys expect their girl to be their girl and their girl only. Girls expect for their guy to be their guy around everybody, they think that they can flaunt and floss their guy off. When boys get girls sometimes boys want to flaunt their girls off. Others would rather keep their girl all to themselves and build or just be obsessive and possessive. When it comes to boys and girls with their expectations, the problem with the expectations and why they're so unrealistic is because they don't lay down clear boundaries and guidelines, and they don't lay down a level of respect. Bringing forth everything that I've said and up until now, little boys and little girls are S-TOO-PID and DUH-M because they have unrealistic expectations.

CHAPTER 7

QUALIFICATIONS

You need qualifications to be in a relationship. What qualifies you to be in a relationship? How grown are you? What are you bringing to the table? People always say, "I know what I bring to the table so I'm not scared to eat alone!" What are you bringing to the table? That's your table!

But what are you bringing to the table of a relationship? What do you have to offer another person? Not who are you, what do you have, not what you have as far as personally emotionally, physically, materialistic things, like I have my own car, own crib. That does not qualify you to be in a relationship, though they are prerequisites. If you don't have those things, those are disqualifications, and you definitely need to be working on being grown, having your own everything and especially your own place to stay. You need stability in your life before you fuck up someone else's life. You can't join your clock with someone else's clock and your clock is off.

Qualifications not only mean financially...Can you afford the time to be dating and getting to know someone? A relationship is a job that you do not get paid for! So, what qualifies you to have this job? Can you get to work on-time every day? What's the schedule expected of you? Can you give what this job requires? You need to understand when you want to get into a relationship with someone, what do they require for qualifications. What do you need in another person for them to be the person that you want? What are you looking for?

Oh, you like when gentlemen open doors! That's cool, I open doors.

You like a guy that pulls out chairs! I don't do that, but I can start.

That's when you negotiate the terms of the deal within your relationship and your understanding. If it's important to that person and they respect you enough, then they will change or sacrifice things for the betterment of both of you. This is what people mean when they say, "Happy wife, happy life!" If you're not qualified to take care of that wife and help that wife be happier with you, then you're going to have a miserable fucking life.

As far as being a wife, do you know what he wants in a wife? He wants someone who is going to suck his dick, fuck him, dress sexy when only he's around, look good when she's outside, but not too good, pick up the kids from school, cook, clean and have a job. You don't know what he expects, what he wants and what he needs for qualifications of a wife. Also, what do you think a wife should be? Do you have what you think it takes to be a wife? Are you willing to do wifely duties as you know them? This is what I mean by qualifications.

Make sure you're qualified to even be in a relationship, and to have that job of being in a relationship. If you're emotionally unavailable or if you have certain ways that people touch you, or certain things that people say that remind you of a negative memory or is a trigger for you, or if you need therapy or counseling, or if you've been raped. There are some things that may have happened in a person's life that can and will hinder them from being in an honest and successful relationship with another person, family included. You must get that shit together!

For instance, if you're an athlete and you sprain your ankle, spraining your ankle isn't a big deal. However, if you're playing hard on that ankle and you're going to the NBA and now you break that ankle, at least they knew you came in with a sprained ankle if they didn't know that, they couldn't have bandaged it up for you to give you that extra support.

Horace Grant used to wear the face protection. He couldn't have had that unless he was honest with himself, the doctors knew him, and they knew what to protect him with and how to protect him. A lot of people wear arm guards or knee pads and that's because they're professionals and they go to work and they do what it takes for them to do their job. Yes, their jobs are a little harder but they put that extra work in to make it happen because they're qualified. What qualifications do you need and what qualifications do you require when entering into a relationship with another person?

CHAPTER 8

AVAILIBILITY

A re you emotionally available? Are you financially available? Are you spiritually available? These are things you need to understand and know what you're willing to compromise, sacrifice, bend on and what you're not going to give up. What's available for someone else to have?

Can someone have your mouth, midsection, booty hole, threesomes, fuck others while you're out of town, are we in a long-distance relationship, long term relationship, fuck ship, situation ship, are we dating; that's what I'm saying about availability. With availability you must know what you must offer, where are you at with it, how available you are. This is after you grow up from being little boys and little girls, and you understand why you are stoo-pid and duh-m, and you're smart enough and grow up and have realistic expectations.

You become more realistic, you have more rea-
sonable expectations, you're qualified to be in a
relationship or you know what qualifications other
people should have. Now you look at what you're
available for and what you want somebody to be
available to you for. Do you want a person that will
be available to have sex with you every day? Do
you want a person that you're going to be able to
see every day? What if you're with someone who's
a paid traveler (salesman, truck driver, pro athlete,
military man, oil worker, fish boat, cruise ship
employee, etc.) and they're on the road for three
to four months, they're not available to you. Do
you need toys, skype, phone sex, what do you need
when they're not around?

Emotionally, are you available? Are you the
type that color? Are you the type that's physically
available? Do you have rectal problems and you
can't do anal? Do you have herpes? Whatever it
is, are you available? Financially, are you financially
available to date, to get to know someone, to spend
time with someone? Do you have children? How
available is your time and you're actual schedule?

Where is your priority level in life with people that you have?

For example, my job called and I'm not going to be able to kick it, you must understand anytime they call. Or an on-call doctor or nurse, you must know who you are dealing with. What type of job do they have? What are their work-hours, schedules, vacation time and PTO? You're going to want to do things with these people. How do you all plan to spend your vacations, holidays, whose family do you kick it with? How available is your family? Can I talk to your mom about us? Can I talk to your dad? Do you not want me to talk to your brother or your sister? Can I whoop, talk to, discipline, tell your kids something, are you going to leave me with your kids, do I have to babysit your kids?

How available are you? Are you available to do these things for/with someone? That's what you must think of, your availability and how available you want someone else to be.

CHAPTER 9

RESPONSIBILITY

A fter the little girls and little boys are grown up and it's understood why they've been stupid and dumb and they're becoming more realistic with expectations, they're qualified and are available, you must understand your responsibility. Your responsibility as a boyfriend, as a man, as a baby daddy, as a husband, as a wife, as a whatever the fuck your title is after you have been clear what the boundaries are, what the guidelines are, what the specifications and ramifications are of your relationship. Now you know what job you have and what you must do with your job and now you are responsible. Now you must be responsible for those things.

You know that this person, does or doesn't like anal, or toe sucking or oral, or threesomes, or whatever it is sexually you know what this person likes.

Now you're responsible for that and if you know that this person doesn't like it, then don't do it. If you know that the person likes it, then do it! You're responsible now with all the information that you have. Being grown is building a relationship off of and with the friendship, you must build the friendship as a foundation for the relationship.

This is where responsibility comes in. Once you get to know this other person, and you know what they like and you know what you like, and you know what works, you must be responsible enough to say, "You know what, I don't think this is going to go well in the future! We can have fun right now, it's cool right now. You're a Christian, I'm a Jew, you're a Muslim, I'm Jamaican."

Whatever it is, you must let that person know! Like listen, "When it comes to us going forward in life, this is how we can go forward, this is where we can go, there is no reason for getting in the car if you're not going to the same place. If I'm hopping on the highway, I'm not trying to pull off the highway, I'm not trying to get off on any extra exits, no none of that shit for you, hop the fuck out while this car is moving, because that's what happens in relationships. People get in the car with someone and want to be with that person and make their lives totally about the other person.

They say, "I want to be with you, I'm fucking with you, it's all about you, I want to make your dreams come true, I'm proud of you, my girl, my man. They always want to big up this other person because you aren't shit without them. So, you invest your life in them because they are already invested in themselves so you just join their train and start investing in them too. That's very irresponsible of you. So, if you put all your money and your time into someone else, and you don't have an under-standing of what ya'll doing, it seems like you have gotten thrown out the car while it was on the high-way and they kept going where they were going.

That's the thing about being responsible and knowing what responsibilities of the things you have. You have the responsibility of telling the truth and accepting the truth. Just be responsible with your time, money, sacrifices, just be responsi-ble with yourself. Don't give someone head if you don't want to give them head and then regret it later. Don't do anything you don't want to do that you're not comfortable with. Don't say, "I only did it for you!" No, No, No! You did it because you were being irresponsible with your actions, your time, your investments, and your sacrifices!

You need to know why you are doing it because you're never doing it for that person, you're doing it for you guys to be together. Until you're able to have that responsibility of that part of the relationship then you don't have a relationship. You need to know what you're responsible for, what do I bring to the table, what am I supposed to be doing, what makes you feel good, what makes us, us, what makes you, the you in us, because you're the captain, because you're my co-captain, because you're the brains of the operation, because you're the muscle, you're the whatever we are. You know your role and you can play your role, now your responsible for your role.

Are you ready to be responsible and are you ready to trust someone else with that/those responsibilities?

CHAPTER 10

ACCESIBILITY

A ccessibility is knowing and being responsible enough after you grow up and you see from being a child which was stupid about how unrealistic you can be and you fix your expectations, understand your qualifications, you work on your availability and then you know your responsibility and now you must be honest about your accessibility. That's what leads to comfortability after responsibility and you know where you are, then you must get in where you fit in and that's the accessibility.

See everything is not going to be perfect at first. But see honesty is what's going to lead you to getting in where you fit in. A person will grow with you and learn to let their guard down a little more. The more you two grow together and get comfortable with each other, the more you two can try new things TOGETHER! It's like trying sushi, "Bae I don't do fucking sushi" but after three years, you try some fucking sushi. Just because you go there with her, you can get you a Bento box while she's eating sushi, you're eating some cooked shit, maybe you only get a Spring roll or whatever, but you're going there with her to cater to her because that's what she likes or vice versa.

That's what I mean by accessibility and being accessible to that person. Once you're responsible and you know what role you play, you must be accessible to that person. Meaning mind, heart, body, feelings, you need to be empathetic to their situation. You must have room in your heart for this person.

"Me personally, my heart has been ALL for my family! So, I don't have no love for none of these hoes out here! I don't have time for the ladies. I don't have the patience for the bitches! I don't have money for the hoes! I'm just on the outside look-ing in! I don't allow any accessibility into me or my life and I don't want any accessibility into anybody else's and I'm able to tell them that. I say, "Yo, I just want to have fun! Can we have fun? We can call it a date, a fuck, you can call it whatever the fuck you want to. It doesn't matter to me and it doesn't always have to be about sex with me, but... this is MY accessibility!" What is your accessibility and what kind of accessibility do you require?

CHAPTER 11

GETTING ON A SHIP

Every ship should take you somewhere. A cruise ship takes you on a cruise, a slave ship, took the slaves to where they were going, so a relationship or friendship shouldn't be any different. You should understand that when you get on a ship it's traveling a distance and it should be taking you to a specific destination, you should be on your way somewhere the entire time. Where is this ship taking you? Like I said earlier, "You shouldn't get in the car if you're not going the same places." What's the destination for your ship?!

We're going to change the car and just say ship. Don't get on the ship if you're not going to the same place. I say, "fuck a car because a ship doesn't have brakes." You can't just stop the fucking ship, you're not just going to hop off the fucking ship, so don't get on the ship unless you're willing and planning to reach the same destination at the same time. If you get on a cruise ship then you're going to the Bahamas or whatever other getaway you signed up for, if you get on the slave ship then you'll be enslaved. See how fucked up you are now?!

Don't get on the ship unless you're going to the same place. Find out the destination of that ship. Where is this friendship taking us? Are we starting a friendship so it can build into a relationship? We don't have to be fucking if we're friends if we're not about to be in a relationship, that's how most females really feel, that's how girls feel but boys will fuck anything and fuck anybody relationship or no relationship. Some females say that they feel like that too but I personally don't believe them.

Your ship should be designed to cater who's on it. You know that if you get on a Disney cruise ship, your kids are going to have a great time. You know if you get on a Carnival ship and you have adults only cruise, it's an adult only. You know what you're getting on and you know what you're getting into. I know how much my drinks cost, where it's going, where it's taking me before I even get on. If you know that, and people let you professionally know that, they're doing their job. They're telling you the accessibility of the ship, they give realistic expectations and how qualified they are to get you there and that they're responsible for you.

They tell you when you have access to get on and off the ship and all of that. When you get on this ship you need to know what type of ship you're doing because people don't have real friendships now a days, people don't have real relationships now a days. They don't know how to have those and they don't have the honesty in themselves and their hearts and they don't share it because they're embarrassed by so many things in their past that they don't keep it real with themselves and shut things out and drown things out blocks things out and they bury these things so deep that they come out as issues and problems that affect all those around them.

People like that have no choice but to make their problems the next persons problems. Know that when you're getting on a ship; if you need a passport, your vaccinations, what is it exactly that you need to get on this ship. Know where the ship is going, know where the ship is going, know how long you're going to be gone, what's the destinations, what's the qualifications, what's your responsibilities, because these are all the things you need to get on the ship.

Nobody plans to get on the ship and that's why everybody ends up in situational-ships. It's just a situation that you're in because you're bored, you lonely, you live alone, you don't have enough money to pay your rent by yourself, you just lost your job, you need help with your car payment, your baby daddy left you, you need a baby daddy, these are all reasons why people get with each other that's not an individual reason about that individual. You were looking for someone to fill a void or fill a gap and/or fill your bank account! Whatever it was that person was qualified to give you what you wanted.

You're not really looking for this person to prosper in life with. A situation-ship is when you end up with somebody. There's no ending up, this is called poor planning. Always remember, proper preparation prevents poor performance. When it comes to getting on a ship, you already have life boats, life jackets, you have all the safety equipment just in case this qualified ship goes down. Do you have life vest before you get on a ship? Do you know of a life boat? Do you have an exit strategy? Do you have an emergency exit set up?

When you're both getting on the ship and saying "This is where we're going" you must both know. Like listen, if this ship goes down and it doesn't get us to where we're trying to go then what are we going to do? What are we going to do if this doesn't work out? Before you get on the ship, you must know what we are going to do if this ship doesn't get us to our destination, ESPECIALLY if there are children involved! Then you must be responsible enough and be accessible enough and honest enough to say this is my emergency plan off this ship.

If ya'll not going to the same place, then don't get in the car and DEFINITELY don't get on the ship. Know what's in your family before you lay down with another and make sure they know themselves and meet their family to make sure the story matches up! Get to know about diseases, mental issues, twins, triplets, religious beliefs, traditions, etc. Get to know yourself then get comfortable with yourself, then better yourself and then and only then, should you be attempting to get to know another person! It will only be then that you will truly be accessible.

Until you are happy with you, then there is no way for there to ever be a happy y'all because you put the U in US! The key is to get to know and appreciate what you have and put the effort in to keep the attraction there both ways and if you don't keep up with your appearance then gifts but never stop doing the things to please and make your mate feel good. Water your own lawn, make your own porno and keep each other's attention.

Impress each other like it's the 1st date always give each other your best like you did at first and enhance it don't be like the rest of the world to each other be special to each other. Don't let other people bring you down or affect you and your mate.

Don't bring other people into your business or ask their opinion simply to communicate with each other and if you don't feel comfortable communicating then communicate about why you don't feel comfortable. Stop comparing your mate to anyone else in the world rather it be an ex, a superstar, a dream, a nightmare, the best or the worst, STOP COMPARING! There is always someone shorter, taller, bigger, smaller, freakier, balder, so just appreciate what you have while you have it because people don't always treat all their lovers the same. People have the ability to grow, scar, mature, evolve and fully transform day to day. I would say with every relationship but really some people change because of lack of relationship they feel superior like nobody deserves them, or on the flip side, unworthy or devalued like why doesn't anyone want me, but you can't let the actions or reactions, or others affect how you feel about yourself!

Therefore, it's so important that you know who you are so no one person opinion can or will ever hurt you. Now if five or ten people are saying the same thing, you might want to check up with a reliable source of your own! I'm just saying! You should both have full accessibility to each other's lives.

★ ★ ★ ★ ★ ★

Keep your own bank account, keep your own nest egg, keep your ship together, keep your children away from boys that don't know them and that you don't know. You must understand how much you're investing and how much you're putting on the line, and how much you're sacrificing. If you have a home and you have children in that home and people are bringing drugs, guns, all of this, you're risking and sacrificing your parenthood, rights, freedom and your life.

You're sacrificing and putting on the line, these things for a situation-ship. You must really get your ship together. Don't get on the ship without knowing the exit strategy, without having an emergency exit set up, without knowing the destination, without knowing or having a plan, without knowing the whole breakdown of how you're going to get there, any excursions, knowing that you have enough gas, knowing that this is responsible, and qualified to get you where you want to go and that you're available to go.

CHAPTER 12

WOMEN

We're talking about grown women now. Grown women know who they are, what they want, where they want to go and where they've been. So now it's up to the grown woman to be honest about these things once you are a grown woman. I speak to the women to the ladies first because it's ladies first. Every woman isn't lady-like. You need to know if you're a sweat pants type of girl, a make-up type of girl, so if a guy says, "This is what I generally like, this is what I go for, this is what I'm attracted too."

Just because that's what he was attracted to when he first met you doesn't mean that he can't fall in love with you and not like those type of people anymore because he loves you as a person. Now he doesn't have a type anymore, you're his type. Grown women must be able to be honest and be able to accept the honesty of a grown man and must be grown enough to know that they're dealing with a grown man.

You can't accidentally be fucking with a little boy! You're like, "Oh, I thought he was just having a hard-time because he just got out of jail!" Well you need to be a grown fucking woman and let that grown man get the fuck out of jail and get on his feet and get to his shit and be the man that you want and need and deserve in your life. You can't be a grown woman fucking with a little boy!

However, you have your own car, crib, job but you have this little boy staying with you driving your car doing all this and that but you're surprised that he doesn't appreciate it. Your surprised that he's driving your car all fast, he's putting shit on your car, in your car, fucking your car up, putting beats all in the trunk, fucking up the windows, your door locks and this crazy stupid shit. Let alone, fucking your friends, fucking bitches in your house, bitches you work with, your relatives and you're surprised but you're fucking with this little ass boy!

You always must bail him out, get him lawyer fees, put money on his books, you have to do all this shit and you're a grown ass woman. Now if you have children, you're taking out of your children's mouths, so you're sacrificing your kids and your life. I keep bringing up children because if you're a grown woman then you understand that you're a mother if you have children. So, you need to be a mother rather than just another girl with children fucking a mother fucker with children!

So be a grown ass woman and be on your grown woman shit and be able to be honest with yourself and be honest with the people you are dealing with. Like listen, "I like you, I would like to spend time with you, but this is where we are, this is where I am in life, this is what I'm doing and what you're doing jeopardizes what I'm trying to do and what I have going on!"

You must be a whole person, a whole woman, you can't be like, "Oh, I'm out here looking for my other half, my better half!" NO! That's another thing that they say, "Ball and Chain..." I'll get to that when I get to the Truth. Women, be grown and be the best that you can be! If you accept your-self for how you look and who you are, then accept yourself. But understand that the best that you can be is the most fit and healthy that you can be.

You should definitely be working out! You should have you a spiritual work out as well. You should understand if you have a thyroid problem, if you have diabetes, sickle cell, or if any of these things are genetically in your family, a possibility that you could be having it or even getting it, you need to be honest with yourself and this man. You need to know about yourself, your blood, your his-tory, your family, know who you are in order to have a man. You need to be a full-grown woman before you can actually deal with a man. That's part of being a grown woman is getting a man instead of getting a little boy. When you're a real grown woman, you shouldn't accept any little boys!

★ ★ ★ ★ ★ ★

Once I saved a pregnant lady from a burning building but the point to this story is that the baby dad, Fred was married to the pregnant girl's aunt first, LOL. He married her, then got her niece pregnant... In my opinion, nobody was grown in this situation and now a beautiful, innocent angel is here in the world!

Whenever people end up anywhere, that's not where they planned to be, so I hate hearing people attempt to explain how they "ended up" married or "ended up" having kids! I don't believe that people only job in life is to have kids and/or get married, and if that's the only goal and legacy they plan on leaving then I hope they already have money or else they are wasting their potential because everyone can be great at something, make it happen! Grown women should know This, YOU'RE a lot more than just a baby factory and servant station!

Grown women support and educate their men, but some grown women don't know this... Some convicts and feloms say they have problems getting jobs. There are employers with federal bonding insurance that get paid more for hiring felons. College is actually free to go now in America. My point for the GROWN women is If ya'll not going to the same place, then get out the car and don't even go to the ship! Uncle C and Natalie thought she was Puerto Rican but after having two kids together and those kids getting grown, they later found out that they were German and some other shit, my point is that they reproduced without knowing their own lineage and background.

How can you give yourself when you don't know what you're giving?! Know who/what you are before bringing someone else into your bull-shit! Do twins run in your family, sickle cell, diabetes, anemia, psoriasis, etc.?!

You put the "U" in us; you can't truly make anyone else happy until you are yourself! Girls always want to tell the boys about other people and boys always compare their girls and relationships to other peoples. There is always someone out there who looks better and freakier.

The truth is what any person does for one don't mean they'll do for another so tales of the X are irrelevant because you only get one side. The key is to get to know and appreciate the one you're with.

Be each other's fantasy, go out of your way like when you first were trying to impress them.

Be the one you were to get each other, that same representative!

TT Nita (RIP) 19 fresh, out her parent's crib moves in with us to be with my alcoholic, dope fiend, try anything, of an uncle who of course is a conman and has already dropped out of college and the military, plus married and divorced by 21! She never had a chance, now two kids later almost two decades later, she's at a police station trying to explain how she didn't kill this white man and it really was suicide because she's known to get violent with men now after the bullshit that this beautiful lady went through because of relationships SMH....RIP!

Sco was my baby brother's dad who caught the 25 in prison on his first case. Mom and De never had a chance! Relationships are just not worth it, and it will fuck your whole life up and so will kids if there is no grown woman involved!

CHAPTER 13

MEN

As a man, a fully-grown man, you know if you're a Titty man, an Ass man, you know if you like this or like that or whatever, you know what you like, you know what you're on. You know who you are, you have your shit together, you know where your kids are if you have some, if you don't have any, you have your retirement plan put together, you're ready to buy a house if you already have a house, then you want the lady to make it her home.

You know if you want a stand-up lady that's going to be working her own job, or you know if you want a supportive lady that will just help you out on your shit. Any way it goes, you have it understood that you know what you want to do and you know who you are and you know what you like. That way you won't waste your time and accept something you don't want as a man. As a man, you can't say, "I got stuck with this shit!"

You are a grown as man, you didn't get stuck with anything! You choose what you want and you work for it. You're a man, you work for that fucking relationship! You protect, provide as a man for a relationship. If you're grown, then handle your business! She's supposed to nurture and support it. Real men protect and handle their business.

Don't ever take advantage of a little girl. If you see a girl being a little girl, help her grow up and be a friend to her, that's all about being a man and understanding your role as a grown man. Females are emotional, understand that, it's doesn't matter if they're little girls or grown women! Don't take advantage of those emotions and don't get them hot and bothered just to be running psychological games!

Just understand who you are as a man, understand what you are doing, understand when girls are falling for you and you're like, "Yo, take me as I am" and you must let them know and nip shit in the bud as the man. You can't be out here flirting with little girls! It's one thing to be nice, courteous and polite but you represent that woman just like you want that woman to represent you. As a man you should be able to have your shit together and keep your chin up, stand tall and handle your business.

CHAPTER 14

TRUTH

Being of adult age, we all just do what we know but the problem with that is most of us got to know our first loves and/or child's other parent first and the most! So, what ends up happening is we think the opposite sex likes to be treated, talked to, touched, and loved the same way because that's all we know. This is why it's imperative to get to know yourself and the person you plan on being with.

Therefore, dating is important. Not sexing, fucking, kicking it or whatever dumb ass phrases it is now. That's how you end up in situationships. Also, by needing something and being with people to come up off them and/or learn from them. Ya'll should learn together while sharing your wisdom and experiences learning and growing together.

Interracial girls and boys, where and when I was growing up there were mostly black boys that didn't have their fathers in the household. There were no examples of men in leadership or gentelmanhood. White girls usually had both parents and the mom stayed at home taking care of the house and kids and catered to the husband. White girls have no real independent white female role models.

** Amelia **

No white woman has been celebrated in America more than her husband or male counterpart Never outshine the master is the 1st rule in the book *48 Laws of Power.* White women know how to please a man! (Not saying black or other women don't, I'm only speaking on American white women in comparison to American black men.) Opposites make them attract and curiosity keeps them interested because it's always something new to learn about each other's past, upbringing and current situations and beliefs. With such different backgrounds, conversations and life experiences can be a lot more intriguing.

White boys and black girls both feel empowered by being with each other for the same sad American bleached brainwashing reason. Sometimes the first person to be interested in a relationship is the last to commit to it, and that gap in original commitment comes back to haunt them later — whether it be two-timing, dating others, actual sex or just getting numbers.

How you start off the relationship is how its going to go until you both go back to the drawing board and get a new communication and identity. List pros and cons then both agree to commit to a new understanding but never think that the time equates to actions and/or developmental growth. Evolution is not automatic.

Guys are immediately attracted to the physical. The better the friendship, the better the relationship. Get to know the person you are dealing with. Girls want a man, boys want pussy. Girls want stability, boys want fun. Stop being contradictory when talking about others when you have the flaws because you put yourself in position to be judged the same.

Boys expect to get with girls that have things that they don't, such as cars, jobs, cribs, etc. There are no bases anymore; hugs, kisses, groping, sex. No preservation, conversation, truth, sex, courting, meeting the family, etc. Bring that back!

Get to know each other's family to see where they come from and where they learn what they know, see who cares about each other and how they are known because you must be grounded in reality and TRUTH!

Men and women get married, start a family, handle their business and do right by GOD. Boyz and girlz are stupid and dumb for fucking and sucking on strangers and being reckless with their time, love, money, body and life.

GOD said, "Findeth a wife, findeth a good thing" and good things come to those who wait because all that GOD made was "good."

People are now appreciative for each other's help and in debt of gratitude to each other but where is the love?! You have to love yourself to be happy with/by yourself BEFORE it's even possible to truly be in love and truthfully be happy.

Girlz want to marry certain types of boys; ball players, lawyers, doctors, kids or no kids. Higher your self image and appreciation then higher your standards. This is how you "step your game up" in life, happiness, and TRUTH!

Boyz are not getting advice from men. Girlz can't see a man because they don't know any therefore they won't have one and girlz take advice from other girlz who are their "friends" but not females in their same situations so bad inexperienced ill advisors most of the time. TRUTH is everybody is an individual and only you two know about you two so only you two should be talking to you two about you two!

Without commitments you're spreading yourself too thin and not giving your all. Get to know yourself better. Like yourself, love yourself and then be able to introduce yourself to offer/give yourself.

You should always be able to reward your children for good behavior and good grades plus on holidays and other special occasions. A child not rewarded can never appreciate or understand the lesson in working.

Boyz lay down for an appropriate time but girlz are responsible for what happens after so plan before. Girlz get eight chances (various times to make their own choice) to not have to be a mother; birth control, swallowing, anal, condoms, female condoms, morning after pill, abortion and then adoption. Boyz get the call and if the girl DECIDES to keep it THEN the boy MUST be a father and is LEGALLY held accountable and responsible. You think it's going to change? Definitely not as much as you are or you think he's supposed to. Don't make bad choices then just try to deal with it when you could have planned better. Grow The Fuck Up!

You can't help anybody until you know yourself. You must work on being the best you that you can be then and only then can you bring someone to the table. You can't help anyone until you help yourself. Invest in yourself does not only mean going shopping but working out and getting edu-cated as well, try meditation sometime.

If everything you know and like about some-one has nothing to do with you, then you don't have a relationship. Get to know each other's fam-ilies before sex. Take time to get to know who you're dealing with before getting involved.

Don't look for or at a romantic relationship for financial answers or gain. (That's just being a hoe and or leech) Get to where you want to be, then invite somebody in. Invest in yourself! Dress for the job you want, not the job you have. Meaning be the adult spouse you want to plan to be and are going to be to her or him. Don't switch it up. Stay solid and stand for something or fall for anything.

Live by GOD's rules and HE'LL provide you with all you need including a mate. Don't expect a mate, get to know people without sexual intentions. If all you like about a person is how they look, and all you know is what they have told you about their past, then you don't know them. Now as a person, you just know a little bit about them which is not enough to be laying up with or planning a future with. Get to know people for who they are and not right now and then dig into their past to find out why. The way someone treats another person has no basis of how they'll treat you. Get to know the person's family and or at least their full name before sex too!

★ ★ ★ ★ ★ ★

The real reason why GIRLZ are S-TOO-PID and BOYZ are DUH-M is because you have to be a real grown up first of all. You have to be self-conscious and be an aware adult to be qualified to even be considered to enter into a relationship. Lastly, after being a fully grown, self-conscious, aware adult, you must build a foundation on friendship with another fully grown, self-conscious, aware adult.

The truth is we've been prewired to be against each other. To understand is the battle of the sexes, "Men are from Mars and women are from Venus and girls and boys have cooties." We have been separated our whole lives and taught and trained to be against each other and that's one thing that needs to stop. We need to understand that we're all human beings, we're all individuals and we all need to love each other regardless of sex. When no sex is involved is when we really get to know each other which is a part of being a grown up.

When you're a grown man and grown woman, you should love yourself and accept yourself and know who you are and love other people. Love people enough to care about them to say, "I would fuck your life up so I can't fuck with you and you would fuck my life up so I don't want to fuck with you!" This cuts down bs so no one would be wasting time with people. You know who you can be friends with, you know who you can be cool with, you know who freaky and you know who is this and who is that. You know when you are accessible to do things with people.

You must understand that you must shake off that hypnosis that was put on you as Americans, because you won't get anywhere unless you do that first. You must understand that you're not the prior generation, you can't listen to someone else about what you should do with your heart. You must be honest about who you are and what you want and then GOD will lead you, your heart will lead you, your mind will lead you and everything will be aligned and synced in getting you to where you want to go on your ship. You will get to your destination if you know what it is.

Proper preparation prevents poor performance! You must be ready to get on that ship before you get on it. Stay ready and you'll never have to get ready! They say that luck is when opportunity meets preparation! Know the destination, have your emergency plan, and your personal emergency exit, and have realistic expectations of other people and make sure you're qualified and available and you're going to be responsible and accessible to get on that ship. Once grown women are dealing with grown men then that's when you can all tell the truth and accept the truth, grow up and understand that these are the reasons that GIRLS-R-STOO-PID and BOYZ-R-DUH-M!

ABOUT THE AUTHOR

Ray Lefty Rhodes is CEO of eight companies, a college educated paid performer, and world traveler who over decades of observing relations between sexes has collected an organized understanding for all to enjoy.